50 Gowns to Style

Design Your Style Workbook

By

Emma Bark

And

. . . .

Thank you for choosing Emma Bark Books

"If you enjoyed my book, it would be greatly appreciated if you left a review so others can receive the same benefits you have. Your review will help me see what is and isn't working so I can better serve you and all my other readers even more."

Thank you

Thank you

Printed in Great Britain
by Amazon